AF691572

DEMENTIA

The Way In.
The Way Out.

Simon Robinson

Dementia: The Way In. The Way Out.

© Simon Robinson, 2025
All rights reserved.

No part of this book may be reproduced, stored in a retrieval system, or transmitted in any form or by any means — electronic, mechanical, photocopying, recording, or otherwise — without the prior written permission of the author, except for brief quotations in reviews.

This edition is a substantially revised and expanded work, distinct in structure, content, and presentation from earlier editions previously published under the same title.

Revised edition published 2025

ISBN (Paperback): 978-1-918532-02-9

Simon Robinson
www.drsimonrobinson.com

Printed and distributed by IngramSpark
Printed in Australia, UK and USA

Reader Notice:

This book reflects personal experience and interpretation.
It is not medical advice and does not replace professional care.

If you are feeling unsafe, overwhelmed, or at risk of harming yourself, please seek immediate support from a healthcare professional or a trusted local crisis service.

This book does not ask you to move faster than you can.
Nothing here requires agreement, belief, or endurance.

If at any point the material feels like too much,
stopping is part of the work.

Chapter 1

THIS chapter opens without a beginning point that can be clearly named. It starts partway through something already in motion, where life continues as usual while its texture quietly changes. Time feels heavier, not abruptly, but through accumulation, as if weight has been added without being noticed.

Nothing here insists on urgency or resolution. What unfolds is a gradual narrowing that does not announce itself, and a recognition that a shift may have happened some time ago. The chapter allows space for uncertainty, for noticing without explanation, and for remaining where things are not yet clear.

I notice that I am already inside something I did not choose.

There was no moment of arrival.

Time feels heavier here, as if it has thickened around me.

Nothing seems wrong enough to stop.

I continue as if there is still time set aside for later.

What I postpone does not argue with me.

The word arrives and stays.

Everything looks the same, yet I feel reduced by it.

I carry it without knowing where to put it.

Days no longer pass through me.

They accumulate, pressing from all sides.

I listen for clocks even when none are near.

The future contracts until it loses its outline.

I stop reaching beyond today.

Imagination becomes an effort I cannot sustain.

People remain close, yet unreachable.

Their voices arrive late, softened by distance.

I answer without fully meeting them.

I hold fragments of who I was.

They feel borrowed, not owned.

I wear them lightly, afraid they will slip away.

Old rooms remain intact.

I return to them because they do not change.

Nothing new seems willing to stay.

Voices feel familiar but unkind.

I cannot trace where they begin.

They speak as if they have always been here.

I hide what frightens me, even from myself.

The concealment tightens its grip.

Silence becomes another enclosure.

I sense confinement without boundaries.

There are no clear walls to test.

The enclosure exists, but not its edges.

I pause.

Nothing pushes me forward, and nothing releases me.

I remain seated at the edge of what might follow.

Chapter 2

THE movement here continues quietly, guided more by easing than by choice. Attention settles where there is less to push against, and less that asks to be held in place. The outer world remains, but it presses less firmly, its edges softening as urgency fades.

Time begins to behave differently, stretching without notice. Scenes carry on without clear boundaries, and moments blend without marking a change. Nothing announces a transition, and nothing needs to. The chapter makes room for absorption without arrival, allowing things to unfold without asking for clarity about where one state ends and another begins.

I realise I am already carrying something meant to see by.

It feels neglected, dulled by time, but still mine.

I do not remember when I last used it.

Even when the world goes dark, something continues.

It does not belong to my eyes.

It has no edge I can locate.

I am absorbed before I notice it happening.

The room recedes without resistance.

Time stretches while I am elsewhere.

When the lights should return, they do not.

I remain seated, uncertain of the room.

Nothing signals an ending.

The outer world grows indistinct and demanding.

The inner scenes ask less of me.

I stay with what does not insist.

I return to familiar scenes.

They no longer resist me.

They ask nothing new.

The world no longer moves through me.

It begins to pass around instead.

I notice the narrowing only afterward.

Interruptions feel unsafe.

I do not trust what calls from outside.

The screen becomes a shelter.

Scenes unfold without pause.

There is no clear moment of waking.

Everything blends into the next.

The tone shifts without warning.

I inhabit whatever appears.

There is no stable ground.

Something observes without reacting.

It does not interfere.

It feels older than the story.

I sense a switch nearby.

It remains untouched.

The film continues.

Chapter 3

HERE the sense is of arriving somewhere without having meant to. The space feels entered rather than decided upon, as if attention has crossed a threshold on its own. What is noticed begins to separate gently: what appears, and the quiet fact of noticing it.

The surroundings feel more organised and contained, though not intimate. Familiar roles repeat, scenes return, and patterns loop without asking to be changed. At times, awareness eases back slightly without leaving altogether. Nothing here requires intervention. The emphasis rests on the simple persistence of presence alongside what unfolds, even as everything else seems to play on.

I find a place that still holds, even in its damage. The walls are thick. The air is stale. The seats remember bodies that are no longer here. It feels like shelter, not comfort. A temporary kind of cover.

I notice two directions at once.

There is the screen—flat, waiting.

And there is the weather inside me—pressure, temperature, a shifting.

Something stands between them, not choosing, just noticing both.

The screen is empty for a moment.

No scene, no voice, no demand.

The silence feels like an opening I might not keep.

Something in me watches without joining in.

It doesn't argue with the film.

It doesn't clap or flinch.

It simply stays, as if it has been here longer than my role.

Night makes the edges unreliable.

Streetlight and dreamlight bleed into each other.

I can't tell if I'm facing outward or inward—only that the room feels less certain.

I remember there is a switch.

My hand moves before I feel ready.

And as I reach, the story tugs—like a thread tightening—

pulling my attention back toward the screen.

I sense movement behind glass—up in the booth.

Not creatures. Not visitors.

More like two tones the body already knows: one sweetening, one sharpening.

They feel intimate in a way that isn't comforting.

A gentle voice seems to invite me closer.

A harsher one makes the air feel conditional.

Between them, I become careful—trying not to lose what little safety I have.

I stand and the exit sign is only a shape.

I move toward the door and forget why I stood up.

When I notice again, I'm seated—watching—already inside the film.

I try to look back and confirm the path behind me.
The doorway wavers, as if it can't hold its own shape
when questioned.
I hold onto a small thread of remembering, not as proof—
only as contact.

In the lobby, the air tightens.

There's a restless, jangling kind of presence—like a rule that can't decide what it wants from me.

Not a judge. Not a saviour.

Just agitation, keyed-up and unresolved, pacing under harsh light.

I return to the wall beside the curtain.

The switch is still there—ordinary, patient, unchanged.

The film begins again.

I wait for another gap to appear, without claiming I will take it.

Chapter 4

HERE the tone shifts through increase rather than rupture. What had stayed at a distance begins to press closer, not dramatically, but with a steady insistence that is harder to ignore. The world feels fuller and louder, its presence more difficult to soften or set aside.

Attention turns inward less out of preference than out of necessity. This inward movement functions as shelter rather than escape, a way of reducing exposure when things feel too near. Brief moments of steadiness still surface, but they pass quickly and do not stay held for long. The chapter allows for this effort, and for the experience of pressure without requiring it to resolve.

The outside world feels like a continual clamour.

Even quiet places carry a hum that won't settle.

I notice myself tensing before anything happens.

I turn inward because it hurts less than staying present.

The screen offers familiar scenes with softened edges.

I let the curtains close without calling it a choice.

What I expect to see no longer fits what is in front of me.

The mismatch makes my body bristle.

I feel wrong-footed, as if I've stepped onto a moving floor.

For a moment, I remember I'm watching.

The role loosens slightly.

Nothing resolves, but something steadies.

I remember there is a switch somewhere nearby.

The idea of illumination feels close, not certain.

I hesitate, then move toward the wall.

Passing through a door feels like losing the thread.

I arrive and the reason has vanished.

I stand still, holding only the shape of an intention.

In the lobby the air tightens.

Restlessness moves in circles, trying to impose order.

I feel it catch in my chest without knowing why.

I find myself back in an early house—too small, too vivid.

The rooms feel crowded with a childlike fury.

I don't argue with it. I only register its heat.

Something small and heavy is placed into my hand.

Not a gift. Not a lesson.

Just proof of contact—dull, undeniable.

I walk among names and feel an older weight settle.

Grief and bitterness sit side by side without speaking.

The air tastes of endurance more than comfort.

I recognise a bitterness that doesn't feel entirely mine.

It still fits my mouth as if rehearsed.

I hold it, and it holds me back.

I approach a place that burns without stopping.

The heat is compelling in the way noise can be compelling.

I don't call it truth. I only feel its pull.

The noise becomes too much and I fall back into the auditorium.

The rows receive me without comment.

The film resumes as if nothing happened.

Chapter 5

THE movement here drifts slightly away from what feels known, without fully breaking contact with it. Familiar reference points remain in view, but they no longer hold in the same way. The ground feels less dependable, and what once seemed settled begins to shift quietly, sometimes present, sometimes receding.

What appears is met without explanation. Images and impressions carry weight without asking to be interpreted, and attention is drawn into meeting them as they are. Certainty thins, not through threat, but through ambiguity. Progress does not advance in a straight line; it moves laterally, through return and recognition, allowing change to occur without insisting on direction or conclusion.

The air changes.

The dark feels nearer, almost physical, as if it has weight.

I notice my breathing because it is the only thing that still feels simple.

I move through places that now feel familiar.

The checkpoints do not welcome me, but they recognise the pattern.

Each passage is slightly less sharp than before.

I reach a shoreline of dark water that seems to drink light.

The surface is dead-calm, refusing reflection.

A lone tower stands where it should not stand.

Above the first tower, another appears—too clean, too perfect.

It wavers as if made of heat rather than stone.

I cannot tell if it is promise or trick.

A presence circles what I try to hold.

The moment I form a belief, it thins.

Nothing is argued with—only cut back to nothing.

The gaze does not land on me—it passes through.

My footing becomes unreal, like paper under water.

I feel myself thinning into uncertainty.

I remain near it without trying to win.

The sharpness eases into stillness.

Nothing is solved. Something simply stops chasing.

A small boat arrives like an old habit of the world.

I place the brass circle into a dirty palm without ceremony.

The water accepts the exchange and stays dark.

At the base of the tower, light ends abruptly.

The doorway is not ominous—only complete.

I step into a place with no senses to reassure me.

Nothing happens, and it feels endless.

Then it feels like a blink.

Time becomes a soft, unreliable measure.

A sound moves toward me through the dark.

Instinct rises before thought.

I do not see what it is—only that it is near, and heavy.

A spiral resolves out of nothing, as if the dark remembers structure.

At a doorway, a guarding presence holds the threshold.

Past, present, future feel like three pressures, not three heads.

A hall opens—vast, quiet, without threat.

An ancient presence waits, tired of being feared.

I sit, and the room does not hurry me.

With each return, the heaviness changes shape.

What felt ancient becomes smaller, quieter, less burdened.

At last, only an egg remains in the stillness—

unannounced, undecorated.

Chapter 6

HERE the movement shifts toward holding and shaping what has been carried loosely until now. Structure appears not as an answer, but as something required to keep things manageable. Attention draws inward and tightens, offering protection while also limiting what can move freely.

This narrowing brings mixed effects. It steadies and constrains at the same time, creating a sense of being held rather than released. Alongside this firmness, another quality becomes noticeable: a quiet space that does not explain itself, and a steadiness that does not resolve into certainty. The chapter stays with this balance, describing not escape, but the ongoing work of remaining afloat without demanding clarity or closure.

I feel split between what seems real and what I'm imagining.

The overlap is tiring.

Sometimes I can't tell which one I'm answering.

I move through days inside something I rarely notice.

Only when it falters do I remember it exists.

I register the vessel by its strain.

To focus, I narrow myself and exclude everything else.

The narrowing has become a habit.

It feels like safety until it feels like a cage.

What once helped me stand up now makes me refuse to bend.

I feel the stiffening before I name it.

It settles in quietly, like a joint that won't give.

A different kind of knowing arrives—without answers.

It feels like space rather than conclusion.

Relief and unease sit together without resolving.

Something remains undecided and I cannot force it shut.

My mind keeps reaching for labels.

The reaching does not complete the thing.

I picture an island eroding under me.

The old ground feels unreliable.

The water doesn't threaten; it simply keeps arriving.

I imagine something fitted around my chest that keeps me afloat.

It doesn't change the sea—only my position in it.

The difference is small, but specific.

I see an old ruler alone, still wearing the idea of power.

The emptiness feels strangely familiar.

Nothing is conquered here—only endured.

Something I once called hope has drained away with the old story.

Another kind is implied, but not yet felt.

I notice the gap more than the promise.

Images run backwards—pride, numbness, anger, heat,

grief—then earlier rooms.

I watch without stopping the reel.

The sequence empties into a simpler shape.

I curl into a fetal stillness, as if inside a warm shell.

Sound becomes muffled and near.

The world reduces to breath and weight.

In the quiet, I notice I'm not alone in here.

Something scaled shares the warmth without speaking.

I keep dreaming as if this is normal.

Chapter 7

HERE there is a sense of standing partway along without having marked the distance. The earlier intensity softens, not through understanding, but through having spent itself. What remains is lighter and more watchful, carrying less force and making fewer demands.

With this easing, perspective opens slightly. Patterns can be noticed without being immediately drawn into them, and attention rests with a little more space around it. Movement resumes without a clear aim or destination, guided less by certainty than by care. The chapter allows for this quieter continuation, where nothing needs to be concluded and nothing insists on being named.

I wake where I didn't expect to wake.

The hall is empty, and the air is still.

Eggshell cracks under my feet as I stand.

The mirror shows me without distortion.

I notice years without shock.

Nothing is corrected. Nothing is hidden.

I realise I'm clothed in something that isn't mine.

It sits heavy, like a borrowed role.

A boundary blurs and holds without explanation.

Something at the threshold regards me as if it can already see ahead.

Other parts wake slowly, then soften.

The guard remains, but the air changes around it.

A gentle light seems to rise from my chest.

The corridors are the same corridors, yet I notice small signs of life.

Frames on the wall. A fern in a corner. Ordinary tenderness I didn't see before.

I find the one I feared, not raging, but working.

Something is being repaired with patience.

We look at each other, and the need to fight does not arrive.

I pass the lead to him without ceremony.

The meaning lands quietly: they will not be alone again.

I don't name what this changes. I only feel it.

I step into cold water and it numbs me cleanly.

The crossing happens without bargaining.

My limbs feel younger in the simple effort of moving forward.

He watches me as if I shouldn't be possible.

Where the blade was, there is something softer.

The gaze remains, but it no longer cuts.

The burning place is no longer only burning.

It looks tended, like a garden that learned heat without panic.

A cool vial is offered, and inside it fire stays contained.

In a small house, faces look back without bitterness.

The air is steady, as if grief has stopped arguing for now.

A quiet settles so deeply I can't name it.

In the toy-room, the child is absent.

The heat has left the corners.

Only an album remains, open to scenes I'd forgotten existed.

The old landscape looks different as I pass back through it.

I feel the ache of leaving something terrible and beautiful.

The road recedes, and I don't try to summarise it.

They greet me altered but recognisable.

I sit down holding what I've carried back.

The screen lights, and the first frame arrives—quietly, like a fact.

Chapter 8

THE movement at this point opens outward instead of breaking free. Awareness becomes more active and finely tuned, picking up on subtleties that might previously have passed unnoticed. This widening brings sensitivity as well as vulnerability, where perception feels sharper and more easily unsettled.

Patterns begin to emerge quickly and can feel heavier than expected. The distinction between inner experience and the outer world grows less stable, calling for greater care in how attention rests. Nothing here needs to be interpreted or resolved. The chapter asks only for slowness, allowing what appears to be met gently, without haste or the need to decide what it means.

I turn my attention toward death and feel the air change.

It stops being an idea and becomes a nearness.

Not a threat—just a gravity I can't talk my way around.

I picture my funeral and it splits into two versions.

In one, there are people. In the other, there is almost no one.

Both feel possible, and neither will stay still.

I watch a shrouded form being handled as if it were mine.

Something in me refuses the identification.

The refusal is quiet, but absolute in its feeling.

I remember how, in dreams, perception happens without effort.

No strain, no eyes working, no proof demanded.

That memory stays close, even when I doubt it.

I feel the weight of how many people have spoken of "after."

It presses like a library I never entered.

Not evidence—just volume.

I look at what we fund, what we celebrate, what we ignore.
My stomach tightens, as if the ledger is wrong in a way words can't fix.
The feeling is not moral victory—just nausea and sadness.

I notice how hard it is to say these things out loud.

Even in my own mind, something flinches and looks away.

The silence feels practiced.

Control feels like my hands closing around air.

The tighter I grip, the more frightened I become.

Nothing solidifies; only tension does.

I sense that the only honest movement left is release.

Not triumph—just unclenching.

The feeling is small, and still frightening.

I look ahead and the last stage feels blank.

Like a room with the furniture removed.

The emptiness doesn't argue; it just waits.

I see myself shrinking around what I can still possess.

Coins become louder than people.

Loneliness sits nearby like a familiar object I don't choose, yet keep.

I watch the mourners and wonder what they truly remember.

I can't hide inside that question.

Memory feels like smoke—present, shifting, ungraspable.

I feel the vessel tipping and taking on water.

Sound becomes a rush that crowds everything else out.

Panic gathers without asking permission.

I let one thing go and keep one thing close.

The water is cold and real.

I move away without calling it courage, only movement.

Chapter 9

THE movement now draws closer to what feels simple, and that closeness brings unease rather than comfort. Structures that once gave shape begin to loosen, creating more openness than support. What remains is not absence, but a lighter framing where less is held in place.

Meaning thins without vanishing, and orientation depends less on certainty than on balance. What appears cannot be grasped without changing it, and holding too tightly adds strain rather than clarity. The chapter allows for staying with this simplicity without claiming it, letting things remain as they are, and permitting presence without ownership or resolution.

My hands feel strangely empty.

Being lost is frightening, and also—briefly—lighter.

I float with nothing to prove I'm going anywhere.

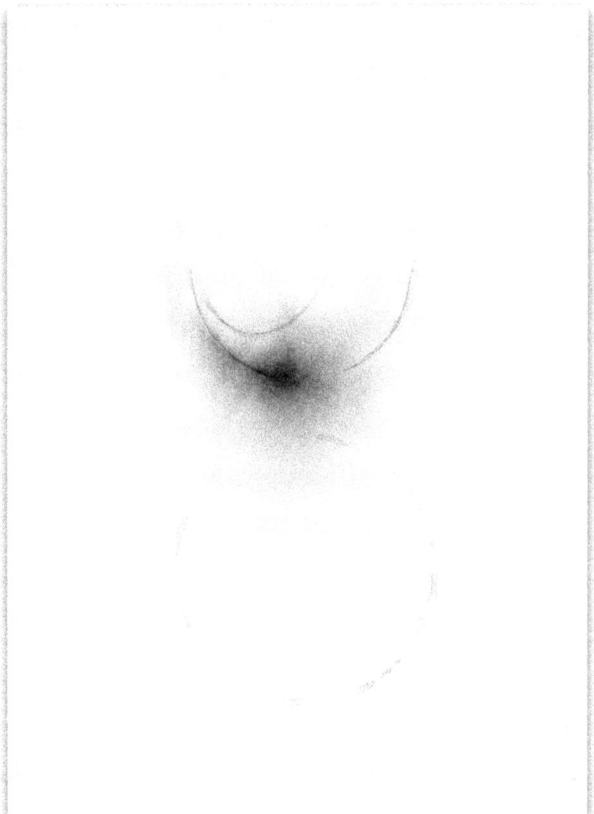

I notice the pauses first.

Then the spaces start swallowing the sentences.

Meaning doesn't vanish all at once—it thins.

I sense the structure that used to hold me in shape.

It feels strained, as if bolts have loosened.

I keep moving, but the frame complains.

Without other people, the noise inside becomes louder.

A small room appears in me, with the door shut.

I sit in it and wait for something external to arrive.

I look back at what I called myself.

It feels like wreckage I'm still trying to wear.

I turn away without declaring what that means.

The water carries me without asking where I'm going.

My light stays with me, steady.

I don't steer. I continue.

Something glittering appears above the horizon.

It looks like a destination and a mirage at once.

It doesn't come closer, yet it keeps my attention.

The air turns cold and still.

In the centre is something that won't move, won't soften.

The cold feels like a decision made long ago.

I stop pretending I'm only an observer.

I let it look like me.

The distance collapses without fanfare.

I feel how easily I lie to keep myself upright.

The one honest thing I can touch is not knowing.

I stand on that, without calling it safety.

I imagine a small warning-song living inside my chest.

Not comfort—signal.

Quiet, persistent, easy to ignore.

I pour heat into the frozen place.

Steam lifts in a slow white breath.

Nothing dramatic—only thaw, and the soundlessness of it.

I notice my heart as if hearing it from far away.

The world doesn't clarify—yet I'm not drifting blind.

Something inside me now points, even if it won't say where.

I settle into stillness.

The dark thins slightly, as if morning is a rumour.

I don't confirm I'm accompanied—I only feel less alone.

Chapter 10

THE movement here turns backward briefly, without the aim of finishing anything. What has been travelled through is sensed as distance rather than accomplishment, a stretch of ground now behind rather than a point reached. The looking back is quiet and unforced, allowing what has passed to remain incomplete.

Ordinary life begins again, but it settles differently. Small traces linger without drawing attention to themselves, and loss appears without ceremony, alongside moments that feel unexpectedly lighter. Nothing is gathered up or resolved. The chapter rests with this altered stance, where standing in the world requires less explanation and carries fewer demands to make sense of what remains.

I arrive late to this library and feel it go on forever.

The shelves don't end; my confidence does.

One open book looks small in my hands.

I notice how fast the verdict lands inside me.

No trumpet—just an instant tightening.

It arrives before my explanation does.

A sentence passes through me like a draft.

The room feels larger, and less safe.

Light and dark behave like weather inside one body.

I sense myself as something continually recalculated.

Any solid "me" starts to look like an overprint.

The answer keeps moving.

I picture a heart and a feather.

I feel which side of me is heavier before I think it.

The scale doesn't argue; it simply hangs.

I remember nights when my mind wouldn't let me rest.

I also remember how easily others seemed to.

The difference feels unfair, and also familiar.

A door closes behind me without sound.

I can still walk—but I can't go back to how I didn't know.

The ignorance doesn't return on request.

I catch myself prosecuting my own life.

The sentence is ready before the evidence.

The roles switch too quickly to name.

I feel the urge to point at something—anything.

The moment I do, my guilt goes quiet for a beat.

Then it returns, unchanged.

A figure enters the equation without needing to be proven.

It feels like a stabiliser, not an argument.

The room inside me steadies for a moment.

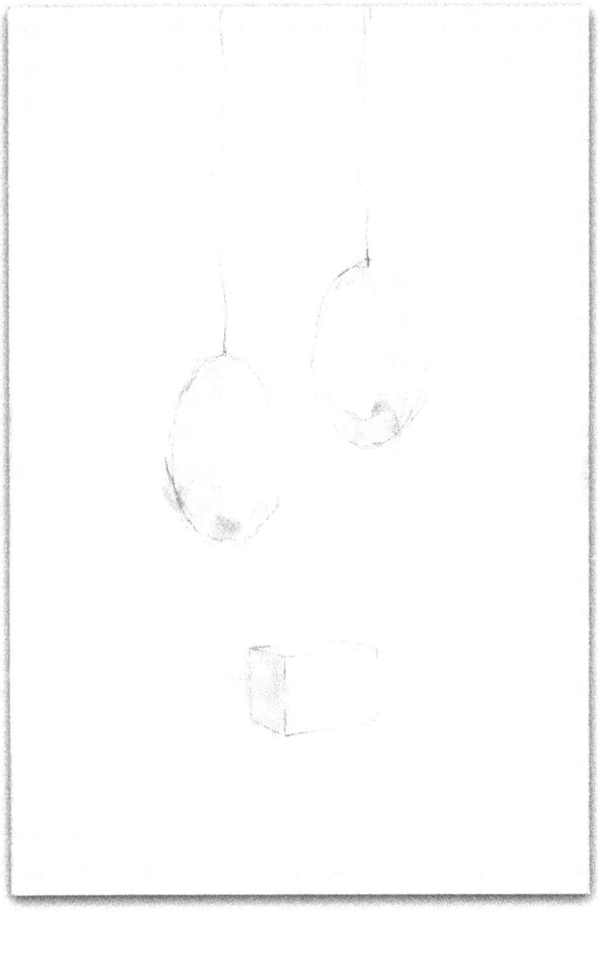

I imagine placing my blame somewhere it won't ricochet.

The heat still rises, but the room doesn't fracture.

It is containment, not pardon earned.

I picture returning after the storm, quieter.

A mirror holds steady and doesn't flinch.

I can face myself without rehearsal.

Something simplifies in me for the first time in a while.

I feel dawn as a pressure behind the dark.

Nothing resolves—yet I am steadier than before.

Chapter 11

THE pace slows here, easing out of the need to move forward. Attention settles without pushing, and the urge to understand loosens into a quieter form of noticing. Words are still present, but they no longer press to organise or explain what is happening.

What offers steadiness is not certainty, but the simple ability to remain with what arises. Effort drops back, defences soften, and there is more space around each moment. Nothing needs to be concluded or named. The chapter stays with this subtle shift, where presence feels sufficient on its own, and where continuing does not require explanation.

I remember when I didn't ask what I was.

Life hurt, but the question never arrived.

I moved through days on habit and naming.

Something overwhelms the old methods.

After that, the old ease doesn't return.

A hairline crack appears where the face used to be smooth.

I know I don't know, and it feels like exposure.

I move through familiar rooms as if they've shifted.

Nothing attacks me; the ground simply won't settle.

A phrase sits over the doorway like ironwork.

I feel its weight before I interpret it.

The words blur into a bar of shadow.

I check what I'm holding: a float, a needle, a mirror.

Not certainty—just something that stays with me.

Three small steadinesses, carried without argument.

A direction inside me lights up as wanting.

The next thing I notice is the verdict forming.

The pull and the sentence arrive as one motion.

I imagine a place where my anger can land without spreading.

A face that doesn't retaliate holds still.

The heat is real; the rupture doesn't have to be.

I feel the loss of who I used to be as a bodily fact.

The old ignorance looks unreachable, like a closed door.

Grief moves through me like weather, without explanation.

The dark presses close, as if it has weight.

I wait inside it, not moving forward or back.

Time feels thick, not long.

The cutting becomes internal—belief after belief falls away.

Eventually it reaches my name.

Even "I" feels like a label that won't stick.

I hit an inky quiet where language stops helping.

It feels like the room has no edges.

Breath happens, but meaning doesn't arrive with it.

I sense layers within layers, like shells.

Waking, dream, thought, feeling—then something that calls itself "me."

The layers don't explain each other; they simply sit.

In the emptiness, a small brightening appears without explanation.

It isn't an answer—more like orientation.

A thin ray, and the sense of dawn beginning somewhere.

Chapter 12

THE closing movement loosens rather than draws together. What remains feels lighter and less fixed, no longer held as a clear sequence or story. Attention rests within ordinary moments, without needing to lift anything out of them or decide what they mean.

There is no position to reach or point to stand upon. What continues does so quietly, without the pull of direction that once felt necessary. Urgency thins, not through completion, but through release. The chapter allows this easing to stand as it is, where ending does not arrive as a conclusion, but as a gentler way of carrying what remains.

I hear the hard numbers and feel my stomach drop.

The mind reaches for certainty and finds none.

What I'm asking for isn't proof. It's hope.

It isn't "out there." It colours the room from inside.

Even ordinary faces begin to look like accusations.

The air feels tinted, as if the light itself has mood.

The ache isn't dramatic. It's the absence of warmth toward myself.

I feel the hollow where reassurance used to live.

A room can be full and still feel uninhabited.

I see the vortex and stop pretending I can out-row it.

A steely calm arrives—clean, not kind.

It isn't surrender as victory. It's surrender as fact.

I grip what I'm carrying and feel it against my chest.

The words that rise aren't polished. They're raw.

I keep moving anyway.

Something flips: the bargaining stops.

The relief is sharp and almost feral.

I feel alive in the moment I stop negotiating.

For a moment it's calm enough to hear my breathing.

The calm doesn't promise anything.

It just exists.

The structure gives way and the sea takes me.

Images fire in quick sequence—too fast to hold.

Then the sequence breaks, and there is only water.

I sense layers inside layers, like smooth shells.

The outer one feels heavy; the inner ones feel bright and strange.

No explanation arrives—only structure.

I remember being young and not needing reasons to meet the day.
The light felt native then, like breath.
Now it feels distant, but still imaginable.

I wake somewhere that doesn't know my story.

Names, faces, customs—unfamiliar.

Strangely, this isn't only terror. There's space in it.

Heat reaches my hands first.

With a full belly, the mind stops clenching for a while.

Nothing is solved. Something is steadied.

A long story opens inside me like a remembered voice.

It feels like being called back—gently, insistently.

Not a command. A thread.

www.ingramcontent.com/pod-product-compliance
Lightning Source LLC
LaVergne TN
LVHW050927210926
848482LV00013B/555
9781918532029